Horses and Ponies

Written by Janine Amos
Reading consultants: Christopher Collier and Alan Howe,
Bath Spa University, UK

First published by Parragon in 2008
Parragon
Queen Street House
4 Queen Street
Bath BA1 1HE, UK

ISBN 978-1-4075-1835-0
Printed in China

Horses and Ponies

LIVE. LEARN. DISCOVER.

PaRragon

Bath · New York · Singapore · Hong Kong · Cologne · Delhi · Melbourne

Parents' notes

This book is part of a series of non-fiction books designed to appeal to children learning to read.

Each book has been developed with the help of educational experts.

At the end of each book is a quiz to help your child remember the information and the meanings of some of the words and sentences. There is also a glossary of difficult words relating to the subject matter in the book, and an index.

Contents

Horse or pony?

Horses and ponies both belong to the horse family. The difference is in their size.

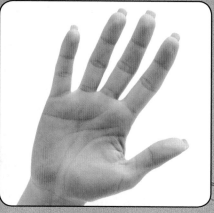

We measure horses and ponies in hands. One "hand" is about the width of a grown-up's hand.

tail

DiscoveryFact™

Thumbelina is the smallest horse in the world. She is just over 4 hands high. She only comes up to an adult's knee.

The area between a horse's shoulders is called its withers. We measure horses and ponies from the ground to their withers.

A horse stands at least 14.2 hands (5 feet) high. A pony is usually less than 14.2 hands high.

mane

withers

coat

hoof

Shapes and sizes

Horses and ponies come in lots of shapes and sizes. The different types are called breeds.

The **Suffolk Punch** is the giant of the horse world. Its size and strength make it ideal for heavy farm work.

An **Arabian horse** is a smart and fast horse. Many are racehorses.

The little **Shetland pony** is just right for small children to ride.

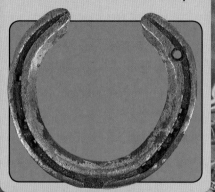

Colors

Horses come in lots of colors. Their coats may also have patches, spots, or white markings on them.

We call a horse with a black coat, mane, and tail a **black**.

A **chestnut** has a red coat, mane, and tail.

A horse with a brown coat, black mane, and black tail is called a **bay**.

A horse with a white coat is called a **gray**.

A **palomino** has a golden coat, with a silvery mane and tail.

Family life

Male and female horses have babies called foals. The male horse is the father of the foal and the female horse is its mother. Most foals are born in the spring.

A male horse is called a stallion. Stallions will fight to protect their mares.

A female horse, or mare, carries her foal inside her for 11 months.

Foals get their first teeth at one week old. Human babies have to wait about six months.

At first, foals feed on milk from their mother. Soon they are grazing, or eating grass, just like their parents.

Living wild

All over the world there are horses in the wild. Many have no owners. They live in groups called herds. Each herd has one stallion and a few mares and foals.

14

There are herds of wild ponies in the New Forest, England. They often search for food in tourists' campsites!

The brumby lives wild in parts of Australia. Brumbies have been hunted by humans.

Mustangs live in the western United States. Some live in the cold mountains. Others live in the dry deserts.

Taking care of ponies

Ponies need good food and exercise. They must be brushed, cleaned, and combed. And in cold weather ponies need the shelter of a warm stable.

Brushing and cleaning a pony is called grooming.

A horse has a frog in its foot! The soft part of a hoof is called a frog. Always clean it with care.

In the field, ponies will eat grass. Indoors, they will need hay three times a day.

Ponies always need fresh drinking water. The straw, or bedding, on the stable floor needs changing every day.

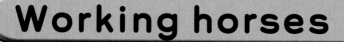

Working horses

People and horses have always worked together. In the past, there were no tractors or trucks. Horses were used everywhere. Even today, people still need horses for work.

A horse is fixed to a cart with a harness and padded collar.

Police officers ride on horses when there are big crowds. They can see right over people's heads.

This photograph shows a horse pulling a sleigh.

Ready to ride

Getting on a pony is called mounting. When you have mounted, you sit up straight, put your feet in the stirrups, and hold the reins.

The equipment that the pony wears is called the tack.

saddle

stirrups

You can braid a horse's mane and tail for an extra-special look!

reins

The pony has a metal bar called a "bit" between its teeth. It is fixed to the reins. To control the pony, you pull gently on the reins.

bit

A hard helmet protects your head if you fall. Riding gloves and boots protect your hands and feet.

Riding

Horses and ponies can move at four different speeds, called paces. Different paces are used for different jobs.

A **walk** is the horse's slowest pace. Each foot goes forward in turn.

A **trot** is faster. The rider rises up and down in the saddle.

When a horse or pony gallops, all four feet come off the ground together.

Riders use their hands, legs, and bodies to control their horses. They pull softly on the reins and gently squeeze the horse's sides.

For a **canter**, the rider sits firmly in the saddle.

A **gallop** is a horse's fastest pace. Horses gallop in races.

Horse sports

Horse sports have always been popular. We use horses in all kinds of games and competitions.

In show jumping events, horses and riders jump over fences.

In the sport of rodeo, cowboys ride with and without saddles.

Polo is the fastest ball sport in the world.

In the sport of horse-racing, riders are called jockeys.

Quiz

Now try this quiz!
All the answers can be found in this book.

What is the difference between horses and ponies?

(a) Horses are brown and ponies are black
(b) Horses are larger than ponies
(c) You can't ride a horse

What color is a bay horse?

(a) Brown
(b) Red
(c) Black

What is a baby horse called?

(a) A pup
(b) A foal
(c) A kid

What do we measure horses and ponies in?

(a) Hands
(b) Feet
(c) Inches

What do we call a horse with a white coat?

(a) A white
(b) A gray
(c) A palomino

Where do brumbies live?

(a) England
(b) The United States
(c) Australia

Glossary

Bit   The bar we put in a horse's mouth that helps a rider control it.

Breed   A type of horse or pony. Each type has certain qualities, such as speed or strength.

Hand   The measurement that is used for a horse's height. One hand is about 4 inches.

Harness   The straps a horse wears to fix it to a cart.

Herd   A group of horses that live together.

Paces   A horse's movements—a walk, trot, canter, or gallop. Each pace has its own beat as the horse's hooves touch the ground.

Reins   The straps for a rider to hold.

Rodeo   A competition where cowboys show off their horse riding and cattle handling.

Stirrups   The two metal loops where riders rest their feet.

Tack   The bridle and saddle.

Withers   The area between a horse's shoulders.

Index

Acknowledgments

t=top, c=center, b=bottom, r=right, l=left

Cover: front cover Alan & Sandy Carey/zefa/Corbis, back cover Horsepix

1 Horsepix, 3 Horsepix, 5bl Horsepix, 6tl Marc Dietrich/iStock, 6 bl Brad Barket/Getty, 6-7 Bob Langrish, 8-9 Bob Langrish, 9tl, tr Horsepix, 10-11 Stuart Westmorland/Corbis, 11 tl Kit Houghton/Corbis, 11tr/mr/br Horsepix, 12-13 DLILLC/Corbis, 13tl Hlavkom/Dreamstime.com, 14-15c Catherine Karnow/Corbis, 14tr Frans Lanting/Corbis, 15tl AtWaG/iStock, 15tr Samantha Coates, 16l Brigitte Sporrer/zefa/Corbis, 18-19 Bob Langrish, 19tr Ian Hodgson/Reuters/Corbis, 19br Corbis, 21tl Lothar Lenz/zefa/Corbis, 21tr Terry W. Eggers/Corbis, 25tl Robert Y. Ono/Corbis, 25tr moodboard/Corbis, 25br Neil Farrin/JAI/Corbis, 27b Horsepix

Additional images used on sticker sheet: first row, first picture: Galen Rowell/Corbis